REAL MEN DON'T LIKE WOMEN

Richard C. Haddocks Jr.

Order this book online at www.trafford.com
or email orders@trafford.com

Most Trafford titles are also available at major online book retailers.

Printed in the United States of America.

ISBN: 978-1-4669-4886-0 (sc)
ISBN: 978-1-4669-4885-3 (e)

Trafford rev. 07/26/2012

 www.trafford.com

North America & international
toll-free: 1 888 232 4444 (USA & Canada)
phone: 250 383 6864 ♦ fax: 812 355 4082

The First Twenty One Years

Twenty years ago this writer penned his opinion relative to the ongoing conflicts that appear to exist between the sexes.

For many reasons, one being the absence of follow—through, this view, which covers many of the thoughts, actions, misunderstandings and disappointments experienced by a male between the ages of six and twenty one, rested in a box of old pictures and reports of various subjects that at one point in time were of interest depending on the cultural climate.

On a dreary afternoon, while involved in that garage cleaning project, I uncovered this hand written, much worn collection of my twenty year old opinions. It's amazing that deep down into the core of all the changes we have witnessed in societies positioning of men and women in the workplace, the home, or in personal relationships; nothing has really changed. I am convinced that when it comes to relationships; what was relative twenty years ago, is relative today. I'm reminded of two of the many phrases commonly used by my grandfather. "The more things change, the more they stay the same" and "If it ain't one thing, it's the same thing"

Prologue

None of what is said should be construed as the writer's disapproval of any portion of the Women's Movement. It is merely an explanation of how a series of changes, developments, and foolishness during adolescence, can reinforce the typical little boy's, "I don't like girls" attitude.

Understanding is the key, but awareness of not only the need to understand, but how early in life this understanding has to begin, will be the foster parent to man's LIKE or dislike for women.

IF WE KNOW NOTHING ELSE; WE KNOW THAT DISLIKE IS NOT IN-BORN.

HOWEVER, THAT SAID; THERE ARE MANY WOMEN WHO WOULD LIKE TO HANG OUT WITH A GROUP OF MEN—JUST BEING ONE OF THE GUYS, BUT; THERE ARE VERY FEW MEN WHO WOULD LIKE TO HANG OUT WITH A GROUP OF WOMEN—JUST BEING ONE OF THE GIRLS.

REAL MEN LOVE, ADORE, ADMIRE AND DESIRE WOMEN—THEY JUST DON'T LIKE THEM, AND ITS TIME THAT WOMEN UNDERSTAND THEY HAVE MADE A SUBSTANTIAL CONTRIBUTION TO THAT ATTITUDE.

Chapter One

The Beginning

Nathan walked around to the back of his house without giving any thought to where he was going or why. He was, however, very aware of how boring the day had been and it was driving his inquisitive six year old mind crazy.

Lazily drinking up the sun near the back porch was Nathan's large furry cat. Nathan's next move was more a reaction to the opportunity to relieve his boredom than a conscious thought to carry out a prank that would be considered deliberate and cruel.

He raced over to the faucet, located just left of the porch, filled the bucket with cold water and poured it on the cat.

The cat let out a sound far from a purr, shook itself frantically and bounded over the back fence.

The excitement of the moment brought instant pleasure that seemed to disappear almost as quickly as it had arrived. He liked that old cat, and now he felt worst than he did prior to the diversion he had created to eliminate his boredom. Nathan didn't like himself very much at that moment and he was bright enough to know that his feelings were a form of punishment for his ill deed. His ponderance, which seemed to last for hours instead of seconds, was broken by his five year old sister's piercing voice. "Nathan, I saw that and I'm telling mom".

Nathan stood motionless. He didn't know whether to run and hide or just breakdown and cry. His sister's voice had shocked him and he couldn't help feeling embarrassed.

As his sister scurried into the house to tell her tale, his mind raced in an attempt to come up with some reasoning that would justify, or at least partially excuse his activities of the last few minutes. It was of no use. He would have to face his parent's disappointment in addition to the sadness he felt for what he had done to his pet.

Nathan could not erase the picture of his sister's face as she ran into the house to subject him to, what was now, double jeopardy.

She seemed to take so much pleasure in what she was about to do; and for the first time in his short life . . . . He didn't like her.

Nathan was troubled by this feeling. His mother always talked about the importance of family; about blood being thicker than water and the need for sister and brotherly love.

The way he felt at that moment conflicted greatly with everything he had been taught. And because he could not distinguish between like and love, he disliked her even more for his bewilderment.

When does it happen? When are we first aware that *love* and *like* walk separate roads?

In the days, months and years that passed all negative feelings regarding a dislike for his sister seemed to disappear, or at least resort to a stage of incubation.

Nathan had become very much aware of behavioral differences between young girls and young boys. And since he was not yet old enough to appreciate gender differences his feelings bordered on mistrust.

Girls were almost always the teacher's pet. And the more frilly, lacey and crisp they were, the more likely they would become just that. If there was anything a young boy did not want the teacher to know, make it a point to keep it secret from "the pet".

Needless to say, that in the 1940's ninety nine percent of teachers were female, or it at least seemed so . . .

Chapter Two

Approaching Teen Years

The development of mans dislike for woman is a process which, after the realization of its existence, is nurtured by the tattling, giggling and constant dictation from parents and society of the treatment to be accorded the "fairer sex".

The lessons are learned early; Like the first time Nathan's mom and dad were told that their darling, "all boy" eleven year old son had hit the twelve year old girl who lived in the next block.

The threat of punishment is in the air. The parent's faces reveal a combination of disappointment and anger and at that moment it was hard to tell which was worst.

Nathan's mind raced. What was the next thing to do. From the look on mom and dad's faces, something needed to be done to cool this less than chilly atmosphere. He thought about why he was in trouble and that bothered him even more.

The girl who lived in the next block was larger and older than he.

She had said Nathan's mother was ugly and he had slapped her in the mouth. He felt justified in what he had done. And since his parents had always been understanding he decided to explain his actions and maybe even gain their favor.

As he began his appeal he was stopped by his father's raised, sharp voice. "I don't care what she said, little boys don't go around hitting little girls".

Nathan wondered what would have happened if he had hit a boy. He also wondered how his dad would have felt if he had come home beaten-up by the girl who lived in the next block.

It was becoming very obvious that rules and treatment seemed to fluctuate depending upon the gender affected.

Chapter Three

Experiencing The Teen Years

Nathan was now fifteen. He liked sports and was considered to be quite an athlete. However, unlike the jocks around school he was shy around girls. He was continuingly being tutored by his friend as to the proper approaches to use to make a hit with the young ladies, but all the coaching in the world did little to overcome his insecurity in a co-ed setting.

Being of less than average height and slight of build, at a time in your life when muscle and superior size were measurements of manhood, served to further diminish his self image.

One night at a high school dance Nathan became aware of a very pretty girl on the other side of the dance hall who was making no effort to hide the fact that she was flirting with him. Whenever he looked in her direction he would catch her eye and she would give him a huge smile. On one occasion she even waved.

Nathan began to ask his friends who she was, but no one seemed to be able to provide him with any information. He noticed that she was with two other girls and the three of them appeared to be chatting and periodically looking his way.

Nathan's friends suggested that he ask the girl to dance and try to get to know her. Just the thought of this made him nervous and his friend began to call him "chicken". The dance was half over and the glances and smiles were continually being transmitted across the dance floor. He finally mustered up his courage and started across the floor to make his move. As he walked he thought about the importance of being a gentleman when asking a lady to dance.

He also thought about all those evenings in his room where had practiced dance steps privately and without possibility of ridicule.

He was sure he could dance well enough to avoid being singled out as the novice of the evening. He was ready . . . Why then did he have that feeling in the pit of his stomach that usually precedes failure?

As he crossed the floor he felt as though he had been walking for a long time. He should have been there by now. Surely the dance floor had gotten no bigger.

Could it be that he was so pre-occupied with thoughts of what he was about to do that he hadn't really started walking yet?

He immediately dismissed that as being RIDICULOUS.

He could see that he was finally getting closer to the girl he had been exchanging glances with all night. He wanted to run the rest of the way and not prolong the agony. He also wanted to turn around, go back to his friends and forget the whole thing. No way, not after he had gotten this far.

Besides, the verbal thrashing he would have received from his friends would have been far more devastating than going through with one dance; a dance he might even enjoy.

At last; after what seemed like a safari he had arrived feeling real good about having gone through with it. She was looking at him and he was really taken with how pretty she was.

His trip across the dance floor provided him with a close-up that re-affirmed the beauty in the mental snapshot he had taken from the other side of the room.

Suddenly he was nervous again. His mouth was dry, his palms wet and he was thankful that no one could see his knees shaking.

However, he was sure that once on the dance floor he would be home free.

He smiled and said, "Hi, I'm Nathan, may I have this dance". She looked up at him with a smile that turned him to jelly, and with her friends giggling in the background she said, "NO.

"NO". No? He repeated the word silently, and as he did he could hear the word resounding through his brain like a giant church bell on Sunday morning.

He felt all alone in the room full of people. It was like being at war and wandering into the enemy's camp. He could not have felt worst if he was naked. His shyness had protected him from this very moment and now he had let his guard down. He stood there just long enough to convince himself that she really wasn't very pretty, then turned and walked away. He felt small and insignificant and he blamed her for it.

Baffled and a little angry he tried to figure out how he had misread her interest. And even if she wasn't interested, it was just a high school dance, and that was all he had asked her to do . . . . dance.

As Nathan returned to his friends he had all he could do to resist the temptation to leave the dance. Although he wondered why he bothered to restrain himself; he certainly wasn't going to ask anyone else to dance tonight.

Chapter Four

Approaching Adulthood

Nathan was leaving his teen years and as he reflected on most of his young life he realized he had become quite a gentleman. He believed in the fairer sex and he found the daintiness of females to be most exciting. He appreciated the different passages of history that alluded to extreme gentlemanly treatment of females. Sir Walter Raleigh was one of his heroes. Stories of gallant and chivalrous warriors held a certain mystique. And he thought of himself as one the many extensions of chivalry.

The inherited responsibility for opening doors, pulling out a lady's chair so that she might seat herself effortlessly, bending to pick up anything they may have dropped, relieving them of packages that appear to be too heavy, defending their honor against non-gentleman like actions AND reaching a point in young manhood where you have not only accepted society's indoctrination, but really loving the role. And then . . . BOOM. A loud bellowing cry from the vocal female resounds across the land saying, "Don't do me any favors". I can take care of myself. I'll pull out my own chair, defend my own honor, carry my own bags, etc.

The emphasis in the difference between man and woman was now shifting FROM; the existing societal positioning which put the woman in the home, off the streets after dark, supporting her man in his efforts to support the family and basically projecting the image of sugar and spice and everything nice, TO . . ." Anything you can do I can do better.

Nathan began experiencing flashbacks; His sister's tattling when he was six, his parent's outrage when he defended his mother's honor, his embarrassment when his first dance request was denied; and now, his total acceptance of society's dictates concerning how a gentleman should interact with the opposite sex thrown back in his face. Women! He didn't like them at all.

Chapter Five

Coming of age

Nathan had grown into a man. He was now twenty one. He could drink legally and had access to the sanctuary of the Men's Tavern.

The tavern was a small neighborhood bar where men drank draft beer for a dime, paid thirty five cents for a shot of whiskey, played cards, shot pool and never needed to be concerned about offending anyone with their use of profanity.

Nathan remembered when as a child going to the store for his mother, he would pass the open tavern door on a warm early evening and peek in to see what all the hearty laughter and loud chatter was about. He recalled that most of the men were giant like with at least a two day growth of beard and work clothes that clearly indicated that these men were involved in manual labor.

On occasion he would linger in the doorway a little too long and a gruff voice would say, "HEY, get away from there". This would send him immediately on his way.

At last he had arrived. He could be a full fledged member of this ghetto "men's club". He had, through age and gender, earned the right to participate in or observe from up close the boisterous sounding activities that, on occasion, became heated arguments that gave way to physical demonstrations of anger. However, these outbreaks were overshadowed by the older men's stories of their whaling adventures on the high seas, their conquest of women and the laughter that sounded throughout when one of them was caught in a lie.

The tavern did have a serious and more functional side.

Men who were experiencing problems at home would come in and after a few drinks to loosen their tongues, confide in one of their friends without being exposed to women who, at that vulnerable moment, might seem like a viable alternative to their problem. This did not preclude the possibility of thoughts about involvement with other women, but the fact that this sanctuary was female free ruled out the possibility of anything spontaneous taking place before some man to man talks could reduce that vulnerability.

Chapter Six

The Intrusion

Nathan sat with his friends one Saturday afternoon drinking beer and playing cards and his thoughts drifted to the first Saturday afternoon he had spent in the tavern. It had seemed like an indoor picnic. The corner of the bar was piled high with several different varieties of sandwiches that were free for the taking. And with beer being ten cents a glass, a dollar had put him into fine spirits with a full tummy to boot.

There was an electric oven behind the bar and the owner sold hot, spicy chicken wings; two for fifteen cents; but it was all short lived.

Women were on the move.

The news media was covering much controversy about women rights, up to and including their exclusion from men's clubs. And although the tavern was a place of public accommodation, the men had always viewed it as their sanctuary.

On this day as Nathan sat in the tavern with his friends, a woman walked in and ordered chicken wings. (Up until now women would ask men to go inside and make the purchase for them).

Her presence was immediately protested, but the owner sold the wings and the woman left carrying them in a brown paper bag.

After a few weeks and several purchase of "wings to go", the woman returned one day with a friend, ordered wings and a drink, and sat down at the bar to enjoy them. As men began to voice their displeasure, these women made it known, in no uncertain terms, that they had every right to be there.

Many men, mostly older, who were very gentlemanly in thought and deed found themselves in heated discussion with others who objected to being told to watch their language in the presence of female company. The sanctuary had been violated! And the men who openly resisted the change were of the attitude that anyone, male or female, who wished to spend time in the tavern, should be accorded no special treatment or consideration.

Nathan was confused and upset . . . Women! What was the justification for this intrusion?

What ever the tavern held that was of interest to the women was certainly overshadowed by the arguing card players, loud, profane bumper pool players, spittoons for tobacco chewers and an obviously clear message that women were not welcome.

Chapter Seven

Nathan's seemingly long wait to belong to this fraternity had fizzled as a result of women wanting to move into a circle that, in his opinion, had no feminine appeal. The tavern stood for everything Nathan was taught to believe women were not. He wanted them out and he would readily admit his motive was selfish. The tavern was changing and he felt cheated.

The old men stopped telling stories of their homeland. And even though everyone knew these stories were lies with occasional embellishments on the truth, they were missed.

Nathan recalled that most stories were centered around voodoo, ghost, superstition or real spicy tales of hot blooded island women.

One of Nathan's favorite stories was of a man who, in spite of his fear of ghost, was crossing a cemetery at night with his dog, when an unexplained moaning sound broke the stillness in the night air. The man immediately started running with his dog at his heel.

Neither stopped until they were completely out of the cemetery. The man sat down on the curbstone, gasping to catch his breath and, as if someone were with him, said

"I'm tired". The dog looked up at his master and said, "Me too". Shock and fear registered on the man's face. He didn't know who or what had gotten into his dog, but he wanted no part of it.

Like a wide eyed, refreshed sprinter the man jumped up with a yell that seemed to trail off into the night as he ran down the street. The men in the tavern roar into laughter as they try to envision the frightened man's face and the speed at which his fear would have enabled him to travel. The laughter continues as the men began hitting the story teller with their hats, telling him what a terrible liar he is.

The stories were basic and simple, and much of the humor was in the storyteller's delivery and West Indian brogue.

Nathan knew he would be hearing these stories no more.

He had arrived at this ghetto country club just in time to witness its dismantling. He blamed the women. After all, who else was there to blame?

Chapter Eight

Nathan had grown into a fine looking man. An as the old folks used to say, he was full of piss and vinegar. The ladies paid much attention to him; even those who were ten to fifteen years his senior. His ego was inflated and his goal was repeated female conquest.

Was this a result of an abundance of testosterone or was it a subconscious lashing out at a gender he had grown to dislike?

He dated many women and always conducted himself as a gentleman. He took great pride in his ability to show the ladies a good time, and he broke many hearts. To this he was insensitive. His gentlemanly attitude and his generosity had nothing to do with respect or general appreciation for the ladies he dated. It was just a fine tuned process which took him from introduction to bedroom in a very short space of time. It never occurred to him that his attitude concerning female conquest could be directly related to his dislike for women.

How long would it take before "LIKE" would be a primary factor in his attraction to the opposite sex . . . .

Chapter Nine

The End Of Twenty One

Who could know that turning twenty two would be like turning onto a street that, although not totally unfamiliar, would twist, turn and completely change the direction of a young man's life.

Nathan had known Lynette for several years. He always thought she was cute, but he was a bit older than she. The idea of having a serious relationship was not an idea at all.

He had only seen her on a couple of occasions within the past two years when he was home on leave from the armed forces.

He was amazed and very impressed with how much she had matured.

One night, after a dance they had both attended they accepted a ride with another couple. The entire evening had been very enjoyable and he fondly remembered they had shared some very nice, warm kisses that night on their way home.

At twenty two Nathan was honorably discharged from the armed forces. He was home to stay and very much looking forward to spending time with Lynette. He wanted to get closer to her. Unfortunately, the feelings weren't mutual. She didn't seem to be as interested as he was. However, living in the same community and being periodically exposed to each other softened her resistance to his pursuit, after all, he was a gentleman and they both knew they had something in common. "They kissed well".

Nathan was aware of some very positives feelings. He had to admit to himself that this was something new.

Maybe his second twenty one years would be quite different from the first.

www.ingramcontent.com/pod-product-compliance
Lightning Source LLC
Chambersburg PA
CBHW061228280526
45784CB00006B/2674